The Little Book of Meditations : A Bedtime Story book with Marcus Aurelius

Cody Dragon

ISBN: 9798370256592

DEDICATION

I dedicate this book to my son Ezra Dragon - you've changed my life in ways you'll never know. Fly high, buddy.

ONCE UPON A TIME IN A LAND FAR
AND WIDE.

THERE LIVED A GREAT MAN NAMED
MARCUS AURELIUS WHO
LIVED FILLD WITH PRIDE.

HE WAS WISE AND THOUGHTFUL
AND KNEW WHAT WAS RIGHT.

BUT ABOVE ALL HE BELIEVED IN
LIVING A GOOD AND VIRTUOUS LIFE.

MARCUS KNEW THAT LIFE COULD BE
TOUGH,

WITH ITS UPS AND DOWNS,

BUT HE BELIEVED THAT PEACE
AND HAPPINESS
COULD STILL BE FOUND.

He understood that the world
was ruled by an orderly
force,

And that we could find peace by
aligning with it,

of course.

To live a good life Marcus had a plan,

He said we should focus on wisdom, justice, self control,

and helping our fellow man.

MARCUS SAID THAT IT WAS
IMPORTANT TO BE MINDFUL AND
THINK GOOD THOUGHTS AND DO
GOOD DEEDS,

AND TO STRIVE TO LIVE IN HARMONY
WITH OTHERS,
AND MEET THEIR NEEDS.

So, whenever you're facing challenges, or you're feeling blue.

Just remember Marcus's words, and what he taught you.

To live in harmony with others,
be kind and true.

And with time and practice,
you'll find peace and happiness
too.

So let us follow Marcus's teachings as we go about our day,

Remembering to be grateful, kind, and to always find our way.

MARCUS ALSO TAUGHT US TO BE
PATIENT AND KIND,
TO BE FORGIVING AND
UNDERSTANDING, AND TO ALWAYS TRY
TO FIND.

THE GOOD IN OTHERS, EVEN WHEN
THEY MAKE MISTAKES,
FOR WE ALL HAVE OUR MOMENTS OF
WEAKNESS, REGARDLESS OF AGE.

AND WHEN THE DAY IS DONE AND WE
LAY DOWN TO SLEEP,
WE CAN THINK OF MARCUS' WORDS
AND LET THEM KEEP.

US CALM AND AT PEACE, AS WE DRIFT
OFF TO DREAMS,
FEELING GRATEFUL FOR ALL THE LOVE
AND HAPPINESS THAT BEAMS.